SUMMARY
of Jeff S. Volek and Stephen D. Phinney's
THE ART AND SCIENCE OF LOW CARBOHYDRATE LIVING

An Expert Guide to Making the Life-Saving Benefits of Carbohydrate Restriction Sustainable and Enjoyable

by SUMOREADS

TABLE OF CONTENTS

EXECUTIVE SUMMARY

In their book *The Art and Science of Low Carbohydrate Living*, Jeff Volek, Ph.D., RD and Stephen Phinney, MD, Ph.D. look deep inside the emerging field of dietary alternatives to combating carbohydrate intolerance, the associated risks of insulin insensitivity, metabolic syndrome and Types 1&2 diabetes. The authors debunk the myth that carbohydrates are essential diet elements that cannot be substituted by citing at least two aboriginal cultures that were sustained almost entirely on proteins and fats, using only occasional herbs and wild berries as supplements. The book also places vital importance on dietary salt as the only major supplement needed to realize complete tolerance to a low carbohydrate diet.

Phinney and Volek discuss in detail the nature of the human diet, breaking down the essential food families, their role in human body health, and their relative proportions in both the base and high-performance settings. In particular, the book maps the energy reserves contained in proteins, carbohydrates, and fats, and shows how the interplay of the three foods can supply the daily calorific body needs.

The authors explain the mechanism of ketone adaptation and how the body can start to burn fat, instead of glucose, for fuel. This process significantly reduces the effects of carbohydrate intolerance including the production of high insulin volumes, insensitivity to insulin, metabolic syndrome and the onset of diabetes. The book also offers guidance on a practical day-to-day method of making a low carbohydrate diet work, including providing recipes and foods for long term use, advising on ways to combat the initial short-lived symptoms associated with the transition from glucose to ketone body fuel, and the signs to watch out for in order to stay safe.

Lastly, the authors explain the role of exercise as a supplement to diet in the new diet lifestyle. The book demonstrates a way to achieve a new lifestyle that combats the dietary challenges of high carbohydrate intake.

PART I:
INTRODUCTION

Introduction

Medical and dietary advice has advocated for low fat, high carbohydrate diets for the last three decades. Science has consistently discouraged high-fat foods despite there being no conclusive, concrete link between fats and heart disease. The time to rethink high-fat food is here. At the heart of all carbohydrate linked health problems (including diabetes and heart disease) is insulin and insulin insensitivity. To combat this problem, this book explains the specific properties, recommended daily intakes, and healing properties inherent in high-fat diets. It also demystifies common beliefs and scientific anecdotes surrounding the ketone diet revolution.

Chapter 1: Overview of Low Carbohydrate and Ketonic Diet (LCD)

Your low-carbohydrate diet is specific only to your needs. Further, it is different depending on many factors including your weight, sex, the purpose for which it is used, and your medical condition. Generally, LCD is defined at the limit below which carbon intolerance symptoms heal, typically in the range of 25–125 grams/day of carbohydrates and less than 25g for patients with Type-2 diabetes. Your body achieves nutritional ketosis when it starts relying on ketones for energy. This is typically at 0.5 to 5 mM B-OHB. In contrast, diabetic ketoacidosis is a dangerous condition in which pancreatic insulin is insufficient to regulate ketone volumes.

PART II: PERSPECTIVE

Chapter 2: Low Carbohydrate Lessons from Aboriginal Cultures

This chapter explores the evolution of diet. Before the agrarian revolution 8,000 years ago, the main food sources for humans were animal meat and scarce berries. The process of determining the right amounts of food types has evolved through a trial and error approach. A Maasai warrior, from a tradition-upholding tribe of East Africa, still relies mainly on a low carb diet of meat (1.2Kg), 2-liters of milk, and 50ml of blood. The typical diet of a hunter-gatherer consisted of 40–50 percent protein, 20 percent carbohydrates, and 4 percent fat. The Bisons of North America had a staple diet of Oolichan grease for over 9,000 years (a fish fat that is a mixture of monounsaturated and saturated fats). They used to harvest sea salt and sprinkle it onto the grease, as it helped ease lightheadedness, fatigue, and malaise associated with high fat intake. Therefore, you can appreciate that your body is only conditioned—not hardwired—to rely on carbohydrates for energy. You can overcome this conditioning and sustainably adopt a different diet.

Chapter 3: The "Modern" History of Carbohydrate Restriction

Fats have been discouraged for the last four decades. Various public committees, scholars, and researchers including the

McGovern 1977 committee's *Dietary Goals for the United States* which stated:

"Avoid Too Much Fat, Saturated Fat, And Cholesterol" (pg. 24).

Most of these beliefs were not founded on sound scientific evidence, but mostly on subjective, sometimes personal opinions. At the same time, both of the alternative diet projects MRFIT and LRC which used low fat, and low cholesterol diets with blood pressure control failed to significantly reduce incidences of heart attacks. Recently, in 2010, the US Dietary Guidelines Advisory Committee issued a recommended daily dietary composition of at least 45 percent carbohydrates, not more than 35 percent proteins, and minimal fats. History, therefore, is decidedly biased on low fat, high carbohydrate diets, despite evidence suggesting these diets are not working.

Chapter 4: Common Concerns at a Glance

Scientists, researchers, and dieticians have advanced various concerns regarding the low carbohydrate, high-fat diet.

1. You can't lose fat on a high-fat diet: this is wrong. Without carbohydrates in your diet, you burn fats for energy, thereby losing weight proportionately and remaining healthier than if you follow a high carbohydrate diet.

2. Carbohydrates are critical for health: this is untrue. carbohydrates were not available in ancient times and some modern tribes still use low carbohydrate diets. The only reason why carbohydrates seem critical is that your body

cannot use fat when glucose is available, preferring to store it instead.

3. Fear of fats: modern science has demonized fats as responsible for a myriad of adverse conditions, without equally publicizing their critical role in human health. Fats generally cannot accumulate in a low-glucose environment, and even if they do, it is not all types of fats that are high risk. Choosing dietary fat wisely and easily is a key to high-fat diet success.

4. Ketone confusion: Ketones and ketoacidosis are terms that are often confused. You may confuse ketones—energy packets based on fat fuels—with diabetic ketoacidosis: a dangerous result of insufficient insulin in the pancreas.

5. Kill the saturated fat demon: insufficient research is behind the saturated fats scare. Emerging research is both confirming the vital role of saturated fats and finding that there are sufficient dietary practices that eliminate the small percentage of fat that is potentially harmful.

6. Feeling faint: initial weeks of low carbohydrate diet interfere with kidney salt balance, leaving you feeling faint. You can correct this by adding a few grams of sodium salt in your daily food.

7. Moderation madness: modern food science advises you to follow a moderated diet. This suggests carbohydrates, proteins and vitamins/minerals. Deep analysis today can show that low carbohydrate diets lack nothing that the body needs. You can choose your diet to include eggs, fish, and chicken for animal protein, as well as nuts, cheese, and ghee

for plant proteins and fat. You may also include olive oil, canola oils, Brussels, strawberries and other low sugar fruits.

Chapter 5: Dietary Carbohydrates: Scientific and Cultural Perspectives

Your ideal diet should be balanced, but what is balance if you are recuperating from a disease, or battling a serious insulin crisis? Sick people may not need the same amount of proteins, carbohydrates, fats, or vitamins as healthy people. Universally, there are 9 essential amino acids, 2 essential fatty acids, and some micronutrients whose deficiency would lead to disease. Lack of a high volume of carbohydrates will only lead to mild symptoms that subside in two weeks as your body transitions to burning fat, with the help of a little dietary salt.

While minimum blood glucose levels must be observed to avoid adverse effects, this level can be achieved through gluconeogenesis and adaptation, which does not rely on high carbohydrate diets. Energy demands of athletes and other endurance lifestyles can still be supported on ketone diets—all that is needed is for the body to become ketone adapted.

PART III:
PHYSIOLOGY

Chapter 6: Basic Human Energetics and Fuel Partitioning

This chapter defines and discusses basic dietary variables. A calorie is an energy unit needed to raise 1 cc of pure water through 1 degree of temperature. A Calorie is equivalent to 1,000 calories (1 Kcalorie), and is the energy needed to raise the temperature of a liter of pure water by 1 degree centigrade. Typically, you will get 4 Calories from 1 gram of pure dry carbohydrate such as granulated sugar. Mashed potatoes, which are highly hydrated, will give you much less energy (typically 1 C per gram). Fructose, which is partitioned sugar, gets more easily converted to fats by the liver. Your body normally allows a concentration of 40 Calories in blood sugar. Any excess is removed from circulation either through conversion into fat or burning for energy—otherwise you get instant diabetes.

Blood sugar maintenance is a critical process that relies heavily on insulin. When your blood glucose levels are excessive, insulin promotes sugar uptake by cells and organs, removing it from circulation. Type-1 Diabetes arises when your pancreas fails to produce insulin. Type-2 Diabetes, however, arises when your body produces insulin but cells show insulin insensitivity. All excess glycogen is irreversibly made into fat cells.

Proteins are chains of 20 amino acids that have three major roles in your body: muscle building, making hormones such as insulin, and as molecule carriers. Your daily protein intake is about 0.8 g/kg of lean body mass, which may go up to 2.5 g/kg for high-efficiency athletes. Your daily calorific percentage of proteins should not exceed 30 percent unless you are recuperating. There are, however, some proteins that have more fat than protein calories including eggs, chicken, lean steak and tuna salad.

You get 9 Calories per gram from fat, making it the highest calorie food of the three. Fats have low water content and are in the form of triglycerides or phospholipids. They are insoluble in water and therefore easily carried around floating in blood or cytoplasm as lipoproteins. They supply the essential Omega-6 and Omega-3 and are the preferred energy source of skeletal muscles (at 60 percent of maximum effort), and the heart muscle at rest. The brain is the most energy-demanding organ consuming about 600 C against a mass of just three pounds. Its preferred fuel source is glucose and ketones, but minimal fat. Ketone adaptation helps your body to transition to burning fat for fuel.

Chapter 7: Insulin Resistance

Insulin resistance is the initial condition in developing Type-2 diabetes. When your blood glucose levels rise above the safe limit, the pancreas makes and releases insulin which adheres to a carrier and promotes uptake of the glucose by cells and organs, and out of blood circulation. Insulin also shuts off fat release from fat cells and promotes, instead, the formation of triglycerides. Insulin resistance results when cells fail to act on its presence. Dietary carbohydrates increase blood glucose, necessitating the production of insulin, which also increases chances of inflammation and production of free radicals. This cascade of reactions is associated with diabetes, degradation of cell systems, and other adverse effects.

Chapter 8: Lipoproteins Effects

You may know that Low-Density Lipoproteins are associated with heart disease, while saturated fats are often associated with high cholesterol levels. Low carbohydrate diets are associated with better lipid patterns, reducing the concentration of LDL-Cs. Evidence exists that high carbohydrate diets increase the particle sizes of LDLs. In addition, LDLs inherently are not dangerous if the associated inflammatory markers are removed through a low carbohydrate diet. Therefore, adopting a low-carbohydrate diet is better than using statin drugs in combating LDL and inflammation problems—especially because they have additional benefits including better insulin sensitivity, increase in plasma triglycerides, and improved metabolic syndrome.

Chapter 9: Effects of Carbohydrate Restriction on Fatty Acid Metabolism

Increasing the intake of fats and reducing carbohydrates in your diet will force your body to commence oxidizing fat for fuel as glucose levels reduce. Your body also reduces the conversion of carbohydrates into fats, resulting in less saturated fats in the system. Cholesterol Ester Palmitoleic Acid (POA), which is associated with Type-2 diabetes, increases when insulin resistance is high (insulin presence, and therefore resistance, is correlated with high carbohydrate diets).

Chapter 10: Body Composition and Physical Performance

Body composition implies the relative percentages of body fat and lean body mass. When you adopt a low carbohydrate diet, a 10 kg weight reduction may typically imply that you lose 7.5 kg of fat, and 2.5 kg supporting muscle and water. Studies have shown that muscle loss stops after the first two weeks, after which you mostly lose extra fat. You may, however, conserve muscles during resistance training (2–3 times per week) during which you lose just fat. Contrary to popular belief, endurance exercise can be sufficiently supported by a low carbohydrate diet as fats produce even higher energy per gram than glucose. You just need to transition to burning fat instead of glucose.

This chapter discusses various methods of determining body composition including underwater density measurements, air plethysmography, body mass index, DXA, skinfold and Siri equation.

Chapter 11: Personalized Nutrition

Your body has a particular composition that responds uniquely to diet, medication, and exercise. Even twins respond differently to dietary programs. Nutrigenetics and nutrigenomics evaluate how people react to nutrition, and how nutrition may vary people's genetic expression. Genetics has a role in how people make nutritive decisions. For instance, different human populations exhibit different traits in synthesizing enzymes that handle digestion of amylase. Therefore, in choosing your diet, you need to be conscious of your body's natural setting to avoid potentially adverse results. For instance, your blood glucose falling below the practical lower limit might have fatal consequences, whereas fat dependence for body fuel (Ketonic diet) is safer and does not require minute-by-minute monitoring.

Even your weight loss duration is closely associated with fluctuations in your carbohydrate tolerance and may vary from person to person. As a result, the dietary research society and persons practicing low carbohydrate diets must realize that personalized nutrition will be the benchmark in the next decade.

Chapter 12: Low Carbohydrate Research Pitfalls

The low carbohydrate diet concept, like most new concepts, has pitfalls. Firstly, its widespread advocacy has a relatively short history. As a result, evidence-based arguments are scarce. There is no precisely mapped recommended intake as scientific research is still building, so that, for instance, it is not known if a 40–60 percent or 70–80 percent fat base is better for the daily calorific requirement. Secondly, documented projects and studies involving low carbohydrate, high-fat diets were relatively short-lived, typically less than 2 weeks. This period is shorter than the time needed for ketone adaptation by the body, and therefore prone to misguided conclusions.

PART IV:
CLINICAL APPLICATIONS

Chapter 13: Clinical Use of Carbohydrate Restriction: Very Low Calorie and Low Carbohydrate Diets

An inherent problem with studies of clinical applications of low carbohydrate diets is that they were conducted more than 25 years ago, and for very short spans of time so that they failed to reflect the benefits of low carbohydrate diets when practiced for sufficiently lengthy periods. Clinical usage of these diets, therefore, is not well defined. You may have concerns regarding the necessity to consult a doctor before adopting a low carbohydrate diet. You may need to if you have a medical condition. In addition, evidence suggests better weight loss results where there is clinical support or group therapy.

Some of the conditions that respond well to low carbohydrate diets include insulin resistance, gastroesophageal reflux disease, PCO syndrome, Type-2 diabetes, hypertension, sleep apnea and mediation-resistant seizures.

Chapter 14: Metabolic Syndrome

You know you have metabolic syndrome if you have a waist measurement of at least 40 inches (men) and 35 inches (women), your fasting triglycerides level is higher than 150mg/dl, your HDL levels are 40 mg (men) or 50mg (women), your blood pressure is higher than 130/85, and fasting glucose levels are higher than 100 mg/dl. Currently, 34 percent of all adults in the US (64 million people) have metabolic syndrome, and high dietary carbohydrates are to blame.

"Managing the metabolic mayhem in someone with insulin resistance by increasing dietary carbohydrates is like using a flamethrower to fight a house fire" (pg. 179).

Using a low carbohydrate diet well, with the proper formulation and possibly supervision, offers a better alternative than using medication in managing metabolic syndrome.

Chapter 15: Treating Type-2 Diabetes as Carbohydrate Intolerance

Type-2 Diabetes starts with insulin resistance. The best predictors are the inflammation markers such as CRP and interleukin-6. Massive production of Reactive Oxygen Series (ROS) leads to degradation of cell membranes leading to insulin resistance. Reducing carbohydrate intake can reduce the effects. You can manage Type-2 diabetes through reduction of blood sugar levels, as by adopting a Ketonic diet alternative. Research has also shown a negative correlation between the volume of serum ketones and hepatic glucose, meaning that lowering dietary carbohydrates reduces hepatic insulin resistance. Carbohydrate restriction should become a way of life once you become ketone addicted, otherwise, your body might revert to glucose metabolism.

Chapter 16: The Importance of Dietary Fats in Long-Term Maintenance

In order to avoid excessive weight loss, a low carbohydrate diet should be supplemented with sufficient good quality fats to supplement daily energy requirements. This energy cannot be supplied by proteins as excessive protein intake may cause malaise. As an example, your initial weight-loss diet totaling 2300 kcal may have 150 grams of protein (600 kcal), and 25 grams of carbohydrates (100 kcal), and the remainder 1600 kcal (56 percent) may be obtained from fats. In time, you may increase your fat intake to 200 grams per day when you become ketone adapted, so as to restore your body or for extra energy.

Adopting a low carbohydrate diet does not cure insulin resistance, but successfully suppresses it as the body does not rely on glucose for fuel.

Chapter 17: The Joy of Cooking (and Eating) Fat

This chapter demonstrates the practicality of cooking high-fat food. It indicates the recipes for cooking high-fat foods such as sautéed kale with garlic and olive oil, cucumber yogurt salad, creamed spinach, French fried green beans, tomato bisque, and wedgies.

High fat, moderate protein, low carbohydrate breakfast smoothies include berry smoothies, mocha smoothies, yogurt blue cheese dressing, honey basil dressing, maple walnut ice-cream and sun-dried tomato caper dip. It provides a whole week's worth of food recipes.

Chapter 18: Ten Clinical Pearls

This chapter summarizes the important considerations when going into a Ketonic diet including your best goals, expectations, what to watch, measuring success, and achieving sustainability.

PART V:
GUEST CONTRIBUTORS

Chapter 19: Ketonic Diets in Seizure Control and Neurologic Disorders by Eric Kossoff MD

The talk is mainly on Ketonic diets' role in improving epilepsy and neurologic disorders.

Thirty years of Clinical Practice with Dr. Robert Atkins: Knowledge gained.

Jacqueline A. Eberstein—Road to Type-2 Diabetes, what is unstable blood sugar, Recognizing an Unstoppable Blood Sugar, One Size Doesn't Fit All, Expectations for Medics and Patients, Beyond Weight Loss

Chapter 21: A Patient's Perspective by Jimmy Moore

This chapter gives the account of Jimmy Moore's struggle with complications associated with high carbohydrate problems.

KEY TAKEAWAYS

Key Takeaway: Carbohydrates were not always part of human diet

Aboriginal people used meat, fats, and salt.

Carbohydrates are not as essential as modern dietetics will make you believe. The Maasai still live on meat, milk, and blood only. The Bisons of North America lived off Oolichan fats for over 9,000 years, requiring only a salt sprinkling with their diet. You should, therefore, approach the low carbohydrate diet concept with an open mind.

Key Takeaway: You may feel like you are taking too much protein, you are not.

Your dietary protein intake remains constant throughout your diet cycle.

Once you commence a low carbohydrate diet, you may feel like you are taking in so much protein (at 0.8 – 1.0 g/kg of lean body mass). This notion is only because proteins constitute a major percentage of your diet at the beginning and progressively reduce as you increase your fats and, to a much lesser degree, your carbohydrates. Indeed, your protein intake is equivalent to that of anyone else, even those not adopting the low carbohydrate diet.

Key Takeaway: You must lose your fear of fat to succeed in low carbohydrate diet

Fats have been seriously demonized.

With all the contemporary advice against dietary fats, it is no wonder that you may feel a distinctive dislike for this diet. You will need to let go of this fear and consider the potential benefits that you stand to reap if you do. Indeed, a low-fat, high-carbohydrate diet is what may have gotten you in the diet related problems you may have, meaning that it can't get worse. Love fats and fats will give you back your health and your great body.

Key Takeaway: Be picky about fats, not all that glitters is gold.

On a low-fat diet, you may have been advised that you should prioritize fats rich in Omega-6 and Omega-3, and avoid saturates. But when you are on a high-fat diet, the reverse applies. You should avoid emphasis on food so rich in the essential fats as your regular fat diet will already supply enough of the essential fats. Instead, focus on saturates and polyunsaturates as your body can burn all excess fats for energy as a basic metabolic process—seeing that you have very little glucose. Use olive oil, butter, and cheese. Avoid cottonseed, soybeans and sunflower oils.

Key Takeaway: *A little salt will be your regular companion*

Sodium will keep you away from malaise.

You will experience certain discomforts at first, including malaise characterized by dizziness, lightheadedness, general lack of energy and possibly nausea. These symptoms will recede spontaneously with 2-3 week as your body becomes ketone adapted. Adding a salt sprinkling to your high-fat meals (2–4 grams daily) will treat these symptoms as your kidney retains its salt balance, and your body will heal as the potassium-sodium balance is maintained.

Key Takeaway: *Don't trust your scale*

A great deal of your weight is water, which varies significantly every day.

You will need to monitor your weight on a day-to-day basis if one of your goals in adapting this diet is weight loss. Beware of taking sudden weight fluctuations so seriously, because your body is mainly water that is prone to fluctuate through such processes as perspiration, urination, metabolic losses and other internal processes that release gases from your body. Weight fluctuations not above 2 kg are not considerable and should not be alarming. As a rule of thumb, gauge your weight variation on weekly periods and not daily.

Key Takeaway: Exercise will keep you fit, but weight loss may rely on other variables.

Weight loss relies on genetics, diet, and lifestyle.

Your proper exercise schedule will keep you fit. But studies have shown that genetics play a greater role in weight loss than simply exercise. Therefore, for severely overweight people looking to lose weight, low carbohydrate diets will work faster to help in weight loss. Of course, you can always supplement with exercise or apply exercise at a later stage to avoid problems of exercise for overweight people.

Key Takeaway: Your Muscles may get sore, and your weight may temporarily increase-its normal

Soreness is associated with fluid retention.

As you continue with exercise, you may realize that after heavy exercise your muscles will get sore and your weight may increase. This is due to fluid retention in your sore muscles, which will disappear with the soreness in a few days.

Key Takeaway: Muscle Cramps—Use Slow Mag if you get them

Your diet change and exercise may initially invite muscle cramps—especially nocturnal cramps. These may result from dehydration, salt imbalance, and mineral inadequacies. A quick fix for this problem is taking magnesium supplements, such as Slow Mag tablets, in a dosage of 3 per day for 20 days.

The symptoms will normally clear within 2 weeks, but you may proceed with this procedure for up to 60 days if need be.

Key Takeaway: In time, your health, and habits will get so much better

You may struggle with the initial effects of becoming ketone adapted for a short 2–3 weeks. But immediately your body embraces this new therapy. You will realize a completely new lifestyle free of the effects of insulin resistance, metabolic syndrome, and the effects of diabetes. You will achieve a normal BMI and your metabolism will heal. You will begin experiencing wholeness again.

EDITORIAL REVIEW

In their book *The Art and Science of Low Carbohydrate Living*, Jeff Volek, Ph.D., RD and Stephen Phinney, MD, Ph.D. seek to describe practical ways of adopting a low carbohydrate diet as a way of combating effects of carbohydrate intolerance and the associated health implications. The authors cite aboriginal cultures to discredit the modern theory that carbohydrates are essential dietary components.

Phinney and Volek discuss the modern concerns and pitfalls around low carbohydrate diets, the fats scare, and the resulting prevalence of obesity, metabolic syndrome, and diabetes among the American public. The book deeply explores the underlying details of a proper diet and explains how one can safely and sustainably use fats for energy in place of carbohydrates. The authors present concise guidelines on how to avoid protein and fat related complications, as well as an all-around recipe stock and a comprehensive low carbohydrate foods base.

The book is well written and meets its intended objective as per the title. It also uses an expansive field of knowledge with 140 citations of works, testimonies, and publications relevant in its field. It is a positive contribution to the field of dietary alternatives to combat metabolic problems and the associated ailments. Though the authors tend to delve too deep into illustrative examples in most chapters, they still manage to present a convincing and fact backed verdict for every argument, thereby sufficiently compelling the reader to try low carbohydrate diet as a way of living healthy.

Towards the end, the book strategically enrolls the testimonies of qualified and relevant persons whose contributions fortify the subject of the book.

In *The Art and Science of Low Carbohydrate Living*, Phinney and Volek successfully bring together diverse contributions from researchers, scholars, and dieticians regarding the practical aspects of adopting a low carbohydrate diet.

KEY PLAYERS

Jeff Volek MD, Ph.D., and Stephen Phinney, MD, Ph.D.:
Authors, *The Art and Science of Low Carbohydrate Living*.
They have between them 50 years of teaching and research in
the field of diets and their effects on disease.

Eric Kossoff, MD: *Ketonic Diets in Seizure Control and
Neurologic Disorders*. A guest contributor whose experience
in John Hopkins Hospital, Baltimore, Maryland helps build
research on the emerging low-carbohydrate vs low-fat
methods in fighting disease.

Jacqueline A. Eberstein, R. N: *Thirty Years of Clinical
Practice with Dr. Robert Atkins: Knowledge Gained*. A guest
contributor whose work under Dr. Atkins helped build a
wealth of experience in writing this book

Jimmy Moore: *A Patient's Perspective*. A patient who
shared his experience with carbohydrate intolerance, insulin
resistance, weight loss problems and prescription of low-fat
diets.

ABOUT THE AUTHORS

Jeff Volek MD, Ph.D., is an associate professor at the University of Connecticut who is also a dietician with above 15 years of research on diets, health, and performance.

Dr. Volek has written or contributed to more than 200 academic papers on the subject, as well as contributed to 3 books. He is a graduate of Michigan State University as well as Penrose-St Francis Hospital. He earned his Ph.D. in Exercise Physiology from Penn State University.

Stephen Phinney, MD, Ph.D., is a physician who attained his MD degree from Stanford University and Ph.D. in Nutritional Biochemistry from MIT. He holds more than 35 years of research on anti- inflammatory diets and has published more than 70 papers in his area of expertise.

Dr. Phinney has worked in academic positions in three universities- Minnesota, Vermont, and California.

THE END

If you enjoyed this summary, please leave an honest review on Amazon.com...it'd mean a lot to us.

If you haven't already, we encourage you to purchase a copy of the original book.

CPSIA information can be obtained
at www.ICGtesting.com
Printed in the USA
LVHW031356131218
600170LV00015B/180/P